Acknowledgements

To my wife Linda and my sons (Allen, Scott, Ryan, Reid and Ross), who gave me the encouragement and support to follow my dreams and embark on my journey. Without their support and guidance, I would not have achieved recording my thoughts for others to begin to understand the importance of the transfer of knowledge and the sharing of these special thoughts and feelings.

To my granddaughter, Taeler Jae, who has become my driving force to ensure young peoples' safety in school classrooms and technology shops. She may be the one who operates the many unsafe pieces of machinery found in our schools today. To Tami, thanks for sharing the most precious gift you have given the world, Taeler Jae!

It is my dream that this book will help other teachers become closer to their students; but more importantly, that it is used in technology classrooms where young students operate machinery to learn a skill and develop a passion for their work.

To Art Fettig and Byrd Baggett, for guiding and encouraging me to tackle this project; and for their wisdom and gracious offer to allow me to use their respective material.

To Bill Hathaway, for his gorgeous pictures printed throughout this book (contact information available at www.digitalliaison.com if you would like signed framed prints). I hope you enjoy it. Your pictures inspire us all. Without your assistance on all the other intricate details, we would never be where we are today.

To Dr. Norm Chaffee, if it was not for you, the issue of safeguarding children in Technical Education classrooms would never have been started. More educational professionals should light the way for others as you have done in Minnesota.

Finally, to my mother and father who are no longer with me on this earth, but will be with me in my heart for eternity.

Jack Podojil

"I Am A Teacher"
Motivational Quotes For Teachers

John F. (Jack) Podojil is available for classes and lectures on motivational subjects and on industrial and institutional Safety & Health (OSHA) related subjects. Leave word at office listed below or send e-mail to jpodojil@fromtheheartpublishing.com

From the Heart Publishing
400 Cimarron Rd.
Apple Valley, Minnesota 55124
(952) 686-2822
www.fromtheheartpublishing.com

"I Am A Teacher"
Motivational Quotes for Teachers

Disclaimer

Although the information contained in the book has been compiled from sources believed to be reliable, the author makes no guarantee as to, and assumes no responsibility for, the correctness, sufficiency, or completeness of such information or recommendations.

Published by:
From the Heart Publishing
400 Cimarron Rd.
Apple Valley, MN. 55124
Phone (952) 686-2822

Printed in the United States of America
ISBN 0-9724201-0-X
Library of Congress 01 02 03 04 05 JFP 1 2 3 4 5 6 7 8 9

My Learning Experience

It all started a long time ago in Cleveland, Ohio where I was born. As with many children growing up, we all played doctor, nurse, cops and robbers. Some of us wanted to be airplane pilots, firemen or soldiers. But one thing for certain, we were all just trying to learn.

School was always difficult for me. I attended a Catholic school and failed the first grade. My teacher would always say, "you are not paying attention" and in the earlier times, as was allowed in schools in the dark ages, she would unleash corporal punishment, not allowed in classrooms today. What everyone did not know was that I was hard of hearing and could not understand what the Sisters were trying to teach me. I just did not hear them talking to me. After an operation, I was finally able to hear, but now I was labeled "a dummy" by the other students, since I had missed many of the earlier lessons, prior to ear surgery.

When my family moved to Arizona, I attended Granada Grade School. I had two teachers I really loved. My sixth grade teacher was Mrs. Dundee and my seventh grade teacher was Mr. Merro. Both of these instructors took the time with me and made me want to learn; and, for that I will be forever grateful. I can say that I did not finish high school, but went into the Navy and then to Vietnam where I learned to survive. After leaving the military service where I made $78.00 a month, I wanted a better paying position. I received my GED and then went on to college. My pride in my GED is as important to me as a person with a doctorate. Why? We both had to have a passion to graduate and had to strive for knowledge.

My greatest teacher and mentor in the safety world was Gordon Jones, who at the time worked for Arizona OSHA (Occupational Safety & Health Administration). If he had not believed in me and given me a chance, I would have never been able to get into the safety field. At first, Gordon did not want to hire me. A couple of weeks after my initial interview, he called and asked if I was still interested in the position. Naturally, it was my chance to do something for others. Gordon said, "Everything you want to know is located in a book somewhere." Everyday Gordon would drop on my desk three items to research. Then I had to write a report on what I had learned. I learned a lot in that first year and today, I am still researching and learning.

The most important teacher in my life is my wife Linda. She said to me, "Jack, you cannot be a prophet in your own house" and encouraged me to leave a large aerospace company located in Seattle. I learned that even with all the education in the world, a person could not help a company unless they were ready to learn. I had to venture out into the speaking, consulting and teaching world and try to change something that was important to me – the safety of children in our schools.

While inspecting machinery in one of our technical education classrooms in Minnesota, I spoke with one of the students. He was building a class project and I asked him this question, "if I asked you 10 years from now who was the most influential person in your life, who would that person be?" Without hesitation, the student answered, "my teacher." This student was building a car dolly and told me about his other projects he was proud of. He stated that if it were not for his welding teacher, he would have been lost in school.

Teachers are those special people who in some way motivate, inspire, encourage, prod and induce their students to become enthused about learning. We must learn on our own, no one can do it for us. But a teacher cannot only help us to focus on an increase of knowledge or skills, but facilitate the process.

It is important to realize that learning takes place everywhere we are, inspired by any event or person who provides the inspiration to learn. But the teacher who guides the process is the vital link. It always comes back to that special facilitator, the teacher.

As you read this book, I would like you to think about one important thing. Who have you had contact with and what learning experience did you give that person? I want you to think of how you can help this person achieve their goals. Help them make a difference in our world and especially in their own lives.

Somebody

I'm not the right height,

And my face is a mess,

I'm not good at sports,

And I'll never play chess,

My grades aren't the biggest,

And its easy to see,

But I'm happy to tell you, I'm glad to be me.

I'm somebody special,

Just one of a kind,

I'm unique, with a greatness,

I'm seeking to find.

I'm happy, I'm healthy, I'm somebody, true

And I'm sure glad to say, that you're somebody too.

--- Art Fettig ---

Effective Teaching

It is my belief, whether we teach courses in mathematics, science, English, or forestry, or technical classes like wood, metals, automotive, or welding, one of our goals as instructors is to provide students with opportunities to become active, critical thinkers. Students who move beyond a view of learning as information-gathering to a view of learning as knowledge-building are really learning. Real learning is transformative. It changes the nature of what is learned because it involves the learner's ability to synthesize, evaluate, and accommodate new information into old systems of knowledge.

Effective teachers have been described as having the capabilities to do the following:

- Optimize academic learning time
- Reward achievement in appropriate ways
- Utilize interactive teaching practices
- Hold and communicate high expectations for student performance
- Select and use appropriate types of instruction

In addition to those capacities, caring and flexibility are attributes which define effective teachers who can create a good social /psychological and physical climate in the classroom. Teachers continuously ask themselves what they are doing and why. "Exemplary" teachers are able to integrate professional knowledge (subject matter and pedagogy), interpersonal knowledge (human relationships), and intrapersonal knowledge (ethics and reflective capacity).

Teachers who believe they can make a difference (i.e., have high levels of "efficacy") do make a difference. High efficacy teachers examine their own performance and look for ways to improve, hold high academic standards for students, insist that students remain on task, build non-threatening and friendly relationships with low-achieving students, set learning goals for students and identify strategies to attain these goals, and expect students to achieve. Teachers who are involved with solving problems and making decisions about curriculum and instruction have a higher sense of efficacy than teachers who work in isolation.

Effective teachers interact with students in a skillful manner. They are generally able to:

- **Establish a rapport with the class**. Most students learn better when they are relaxed, confident and not feeling threatened. A comfortable atmosphere makes learning more enjoyable and encourages individuality and creativity. Nurture this atmosphere by remaining approachable, keeping your office hours, and encouraging students to visit during that time. An important thing to remember is that as an instructor your response and comments carry great weight.

- **When a student asks a question**, respond with respect. You need not spend five minutes answering an irrelevant question, but you can still be courteous by offering to discuss the matter with the student after class.

- **Be open to student questions**. Students appreciate it when teachers are open to questions and willing to answer questions. It is important to encourage students to ask questions and help them to learn to frame questions that get the kind of information they need in order to learn. If you watch your students instead of the chalkboard or your notes, you can often encourage questions simply by pausing whenever they appear confused and even by saying, "I see you have some questions, what are they?"

- **Stimulate class participation**. Students appreciate the opportunity to engage in well-planned class discussion and class activities. Thus, if you want students to participate in your class, you need to use various strategies to stimulate their participation. In some instances, you might highlight important information from their reading. In other cases, you might have them write briefly or participate in small group exercises as a way of helping them identify their needs and focus their thoughts prior to their active participation in your class. An exchange of ideas of all sorts is a natural part of an academic environment and students need to feel comfortable with this exchange, not threatened by it. A lot of their comfort, however, depends on creating a nurturing environment and clarifying expectations for participation.

If school improvement depends, fundamentally, on the improvement of teaching, ways to increase teacher motivation and capabilities should be the core processes upon which efforts to make schools more effective focus. Of course, the motivation and capabilities of other school personnel are important but it is what teachers know and do that makes the biggest difference in a student's life. Effective policies and practices that increase teacher motivation and capabilities can be adapted to other school staff members.

Teachers, like all professionals, require both intrinsic and extrinsic rewards. Herzberg (1964) distinguishes between extrinsic rewards surrounding a job (such as salaries, fringe benefits, and job security) and intrinsic rewards of the job itself (such as self-respect, sense of accomplishment, and personal growth).

Recent studies have shown fairly conclusively that teachers are motivated more by intrinsic than by extrinsic rewards. Pastor Erlandson (1982) conducted a survey which found that teachers perceive their needs and measure their job satisfaction by factors such as participation in decision making, use of valued skills, freedom and independence, challenge, expression of creativity, and opportunity for learning. They concluded that high internal motivation, work satisfaction, and high-quality performance depend on three "critical psychological states": experienced meaningfulness, responsibility for outcomes, and knowledge of results.

" Some people walk into your life and quickly go.
Others walk into your life, leave footprints and then leave.
After that, you are never, ever the same."
--- Author Unknown ---

This fits my life really well, because so many people have walked in and out of my life, but only a few have left any footprints. There are a few of my teachers/mentors that have been there for me throughout hard times. They've made me realize that I do have a life to live, and that I want to help people in the same way they've helped me. So for those teachers: thank you so very much for molding me.

My Experiences In The Classroom

If you would have ever asked any of my former instructors if they ever thought that I would end up being a teacher or a motivational speaker they would have probably keeled over with laughter. Many instructors have a few students that we shake our heads at and try to motivate to make the best out of their lives. Like each of you reading this book, I loved each and every student that came into my classroom. Each had their own special needs and they all wanted to learn and find better jobs.

As instructors, we have followed what has been happening in our classrooms today; and, we know about the dangers. We have heard about the incidents at Columbine High and other schools where instructors have put their lives on the line to protect their students. Let me share a couple of stories with you.

When I was an instructor at South Seattle Community College, located in Seattle, Washington, I had two students I will remember for a long time.

Todd was a great guy who came to class trying to make a new start in life and raise a family. He knew he had to complete his education if he wanted to work in the safety field. Todd had served in the Marine Corps and was truly a great troop. Every other day he would drive from the far side of the Puget Sound, take the Seattle ferry to get to my class and then hurry out after class to catch the ferry back and go to work as a security guard.

Once I asked Todd, "why do you want this degree in safety?" He answered, "I want to be a teacher like you."

Todd always tried his best, but it was like he was looking for land mines. As a matter of fact, when I asked him what he did in the service he said he had, "looked for land mines!" So, we nicknamed him, "Landmine." Do you have pet names for any of your special students?

One day Todd was sitting next to another student and fumbling around in a bag and the other student was looking in the bag. Well it did not take me long to loose track of what I was trying to teach so I confronted him. I said, "Todd what do you have in the bag?" and he answered, "nothing." Well, I knew better; and asked him again. That is when he pulled out the biggest 9mm pistol I have ever seen and was pointing it at the student in front of him. Now at this point a teacher has to be thinking, "what do I do now?" Right?

The other students did not know whether to duck under the desk or run. In my case, I very calmly asked him why the gun was on campus. He said he had asked the security department and they told him it was okay to bring it on campus. Immediately I told Todd that I did not care if he took the gun to his car and put it in the trunk or if he left the classroom and went home but the gun had to go.

Once again, Todd reassured everyone in the classroom that it was okay. One thing I forgot to mention was that the other student that sat in front of Todd was Mike and he was a Federal Marshall. I talked Todd into leaving the classroom with me and we went to see the dean of the college. As we walked into his office, he took one look at the gun and under the desk he went. We finally assured him that no harm was going to come to him and we were able to discuss the problem.

The dean immediately called security who explained there was no law in the State of Washington that prohibited a person from carrying a concealed weapon onto a college campus. Needless to say, there was a choice to be made here. Let Todd keep the gun in class or quit teaching for the day. Well, Todd and I agreed that the best solution in this case was for the gun to go into the trunk of his car. That was the end of that class day.

On a more tragic note

I was out ill for a period of time and my wife, Linda took over the safety instruction for me. Linda was also an instructor at the college. Each night after class I would ask her how her night went and she would say "wonderful." She told me about one student named Lonnie D---- how he was so nice to her, helped her clean up the room after class, walked her to her car and was so polite. I was glad that she was doing so well with the students and thanked her for pitching in for me.

When I returned to the classroom, most of the students were new to me so I went around the room asking names and checking the roster. Lonnie was not there that day and I was looking forward to meeting him. Lonnie showed up the next training day and sat next to a couple of other students. As I was trying to teach, Lonnie was trying to have a side conversation. (Has that ever happened in your classroom?) If it has, you know what came next. I asked Lonnie to please hold the conversation until the end of class.

I continued teaching; and right in the middle of my lecture, Lonnie came up to the front of the classroom and started sharpening his pencil. I thought, "wow is this really happening?" I calmly asked him to go back and sit down. Lonnie came over to me and asked if he could speak to me in the hall after class. I said, "sure." Now remember, I am the guy who did not go to school but went into the military service, so I was used to this type of person.

After class, I met with Lonnie in the hall and asked him what his problem was. Lonnie looked me right in the eye and said, "I really like your wife but I really do not like you." I explained to Lonnie that he may go through life not liking a lot of people but that we must all get along. I reminded him that he took valuable time away from the other students. Lonnie repeated his statement and walked away.

After class, I talked to my wife and explained what took place. Linda said, "I can not believe it, he was always nice to me." As I was leaving the college for the night, I stopped into the dean's office and told him what had happened. The dean said, "If the guy gives you trouble, throw him out of your class." I left the next day to go to Minneapolis.

Well the week ended up on a positive note. While I was sitting in the airport I called Linda to tell her I was on my way back home. Linda told me that she might be late picking me up since Interstate 5 had been shut down. Someone went on a killing spree, killing his mother and baby nephew, stealing her car, hitting a person on a motorcycle and pushing him into a retaining wall. Linda went on to say that the Seattle police chased him over a fence where he assaulted another woman working in her backyard, broke into a house and stole weapons and then held off the police department until a Swat officer shot and killed him.

I returned home late that night. The next morning, as we were enjoying the Seattle sunrise, (yes Seattle does get some sun) someone knocked on our door. I opened the door and there was a television camera right in my face. Now can you imagine what I was thinking? I immediately called Linda to the door and the news person asked if she could speak with us about one of our students? At this point we did not know what it was all about. With the cameras rolling, the news person asked us questions about this student and the student was Lonnie. Was he headed our way? Who knows where he was going next?

The newspapers and newsrooms carried this story.

Friday, May 27, 1999, Lonnie D---- killed his mother and nephew. They were stabbed to death. He then fatally beat a woman, critically injured another woman, ran over a motorcyclist and shot a sheriff's deputy. A pretty good effort from a guy that most thought was a pretty together guy.

Believed to be responsible for it all was 21-year-old Lonnie D----, who was shot dead by a police sniper after a standoff with authorities in a northern suburb of Seattle.

Lonnie had previous run-ins with the law in King County, but no known history of violence, Brier Police Chief Gary Minor stated.

"I don't think we're ever going to know what set him off. At this point, we don't have a clue," he said. "We did not know that he had a history of any mental problems."

It started with the deaths of Lonnie's mother, Sheila L., 46, and his sister's son, Kahari P., 18 months. The two were stabbed to death with a three-inch paring knife Friday morning, probably around 10 or 11 a.m.", Minor said.

Lonnie changed out of his bloodied jeans and T-shirt and left the home without washing up.

At about 1:30 p.m., Lonnie, driving his mother's black Honda station wagon, swerved into a motorcycle on Interstate 5 in Shoreline, located in King County a few miles south of Brier.

The motorcyclist, Anthony V., 64, had to have his leg amputated below the knee.

It must have been a fairly violent accident because papers described the car as being "torn in half and burned." Lonnie fled on foot into a nearby neighborhood.

Moments later, a resident called 911 when she heard Erma S----- screaming for help.

Erma, 63, was found lying in her yard in a pool of blood, with what looked like a broken posthole digger - a garden tool - near her body. She was pronounced dead at a local hospital.

Lonnie then attacked 82-year-old Irene H. in her yard, hitting her with an unknown object and breaking her neck and critically injuring her police said. (I'm not sure if she survived.)

Sheriff's officers say the man then found an empty house that contained a large number of weapons and started firing at officers. Deputy Diana Russell was hit in the head by flying glass and a ricocheting bullet. She was in serious condition that Saturday night (I don't know if she survived.)

King County Sheriff, Dave Reichert, said his officers responded with just the single sniper shot. The officers then fired three rounds of tear gas into the home, at 15-minute intervals, to make sure the man was down, he said.

The sniper's shot was meant to kill. "It's a sad thing and it's a tough decision to make," stated an official from the Seattle Police, "but in this case it was the right thing to do."

Needless to say, these two students have impacted my life but like many of you reading this book, I continue to instruct and motivate students, as it is my life's passion.

As teachers, we should have the right to know the backgrounds of our students. We should know if they have learning or emotional problems and we should have the opportunity to have a safe working and learning environment. If you have stories that strongly impacted your life, I would love to hear them.

Technology Classes

It was for a special reason Linda and I left the beautiful northwest and moved to Minnesota. The reason for this move was to help establish a machine guarding committee for the technology classes located in our schools in Minnesota. Each state has their own terminology for technology classes and sometimes it is called Tech-prep, VICA, or Technical Education.

Many parents today do not know what is taught in these classrooms. For example, in our schools in Minnesota (as in other states) our instructors teach their students how to design and build fuel-efficient cars. Cars that will get 300 to 600 miles to a gallon of gas. Each year instructors across the state have their students design the cars, research fuels, modify engines, and build the cars to compete in what is known as the Super-mileage Challenge. Some schools build solar-powered boats.

Other instructors help the student design and build a house, which is auctioned to the highest bidder; and, then the money from the auction is sent back into the next class. One student was building a deer stand for his father, who was very ill. This student wanted to build his father a place to sit in comfort to watch the deer in his backyard. Remember the student that said his teacher was the one that he would remember ten years from now? Well, all of these students were developing an occupational skill. A skill that will help them in their later years.

I am amazed when I travel across the United States and the same story unfolds. Instructors trying to manage 7-12th grade technical classes with 25 to 30 students in them. This is one of the most common complaints I hear. When they ask to reduce the class size to a safer level or request money for safety equipment, they are told by many school officials that if they need to spend money for safety equipment the classroom will be shut down and computers will be purchased.

Funny, it seems we all have money for football, music, and band uniforms. Now I am not saying that these subjects are not important, but what I am trying to say is that learning a vocational skill should rank right up there. Technical classrooms are vital to the success of our country. If school officials think that buildings, roads, cars, furniture, airplanes, etc are going to be built by computers alone, they need to go back to school themselves since they have lost the vision and value of learning. Not all of the students that I meet want to be pilots, doctors or lawyers. Many want to go into the trades, where they can make as much money as the other professions.

Believe it or not, 98% of machinery found in all of our schools do not meet minimum safety standards.

The Problem

Guarding of machinery is required to prevent injury to the operator and other people in the machine area. It is **presumed** that machine designers strive to produce machinery, which will perform the intended function without damage to itself and without causing injury to the operator.

Today, many well-known machine manufacturers still fabricate and sell their equipment without the necessary safeguards and electrical controls required by OSHA, national consensus standards and various safety regulations to protect people from hazards not associated with the point of operation.

Many of these manufacturers never warn the person buying their equipment that safety devices are missing. A representative of a well-known manufacturer of woodworking and sheet metal equipment stated that if their company installed required safety devices (separate emergency stops and power outage protection) on their machine, they could not sell the equipment for under $99.00. They further stated they have only been sued a few times for this hazard and would rather pay the laws suits.

Would you want to purchase their equipment for your family, students, or employees to use without it being equipped with the proper safety equipment? Would you like to be cited by OSHA and penalized for not having the proper safeguarding equipment that is required to be installed by the manufacturer? Well, chances are, you are at risk for this potential everyday. Today, many of these hazards are missed or overlooked by most inspectors and they end up in your shop or classroom.

A Fresh Approach

If we are ever going to change behavior and culture, when working with machinery, we must concentrate our efforts in our schools. Recently, a new focus was placed on the operation of machinery in schools in the state of Minnesota. Many students in this state and other states are being seriously injured on equipment that was either purchased by or donated to the school.

These machines are the same type of industrial machines used in general industry, but are now used in middle schools, high schools, and technical colleges, where young adults and inexperienced operators are allowed to operate them.

In the State of Minnesota, a group of concerned citizens formed a machine guarding technical committee for the Minneapolis area schools. The members of this group are the Metro Educational Cooperative Service Unit, the Minnesota Safety Council, Minnesota OSHA, area teachers, and private companies. This committee meets monthly and has established safety standards that will prevent machines from being sold or used in Minnesota schools if they are unsafe. In fact, every school in this state was required by the Department of Children, Families and Learning (known in many states as the Department of Education) to inspect every machine, under their jurisdiction.

After the surveys were conducted, the committee learned that even the inspectors may not have had the necessary training to inspect the machinery; and, therefore hazards were missed.

This committee, the first of its kind in the United States, developed guidelines to ensure the safety of teachers and students. The following is an excerpt:

- Proper bid specifications with a safety warranty attached. This warranty states that if a machine does not meet the intent of all recognized standards the machine manufacturer will bring the machine into compliance at **no cost** to the school district.

- A safety inspection guidebook that can be used in the classroom for teachers and students to inspect their machinery.

- Preventive maintenance programs and addendums so proper maintenance is performed at proper intervals.

- A training course in machine safeguarding that every instructor must attend. When training has been completed, the attendee will be certified through the State Education Program, enabling the school to apply for and receive funding to abate any safety deficiencies on their school's machinery. To date we have instructed over 1,000 people.

What can you do?

Do you know anyone who may have young adults (children) in schools? It is time for you to get involved in your community as a professional. Help at schools where they may not have the required knowledge to inspect machinery. Establish a committee at the Department of Education level to ensure that young adults are educated on safe machinery and with proper curriculum that stresses safe work habits. Work with the manufacturers to ensure that only safe equipment is manufactured and sold to employers and especially to the schools.

Optimum machine safeguarding can only be achieved by using an approach that combines safe equipment with safe operation. Following the portion of the OSHA standard related to your work activity will never reduce all potential accidental loss. Many of these OSHA standards are outdated and many times in conflict with one another. A machine-guarding program that does not address each potential hazard (task/risk analysis) including ergonomics and education can never be a successful program.

Please take my quote and if you know of a technical classroom in your area, please give it to them.

"In every school classroom, a student should be able to look around and see a model classroom, where there are no safety or health hazards, and where skilled instructors are protecting their safety and health by teaching a professional skill on safe equipment and in a safe environment." --- Jack Podojil © ---

As you read my book and the following quotes, think about our children and their teachers. Think how we can achieve a better learning environment and how we can all help our teachers achieve their goal: providing the leaders for tomorrow.

Motivational Quotes

Morning Glory Pool - Yellowstone National Park

If you are a teacher and you are reading this, you are a role model. Believe it or not, there is a student out there watching your every mood; this student thinks the world of you. You as a teacher – to be a great one, should look for that student. Talk to them, smile at them, at least wave. Let them know they are recognized and cared for. As a student who deeply admired a teacher who barely recognized me, I can tell you it was one of the worst feelings in the world! Please reach out to your students. They need you more than they or you may think!

--- Wishing to remain anonymous---

Yellowstone Falls - Yellowstone National Park

“Every child is an artist.
The problem is how to remain an artist once he grows up.”
--- Pablo Picasso ---

“ A teacher can never truly teach unless he or she is still learning themselves. A lamp can never light another lamp unless it continues to burn its own flame. The teacher who has come to the end of his subject, who has no living traffic with his knowledge but merely repeats his lesson to his students, can only load their minds, he cannot quicken them.”
--- Rabindranath Tagore ---

“There can be no learning, if there has been no teaching”
--- Anonymous ---

Yellowstone Falls - Yellowstone National Park

"The greatest gift that you can give to another person is knowledge, for knowledge is power. Power to build and power to dream and what you can envision in your mind you can achieve."

--- *Jack Podojil.* © ---

"I have a present that is challenging, adventurous and fun. I am allowed to spend my days with the future of our country, protecting the safety and health of children in our schools. Only those who dare to fail greatly, can ever achieve greatly."

--- *Jack Podojil* © ---

Southern Minnesota - Early Morning

Summertime

They're going home for summer now, my kids. And I ask myself "Did I really make a difference in their lives?" Will they sometime, somewhere, look back and think "My teacher really cared."? They aren't my students any longer. They move on, And come September I must face yet another class of strangers. They're going home for summer now, wiser and richer, I hope, than when we started out. I honestly believe I gave them everything I had to give.

They got it all, and Oh, I hope it was enough. It's tough, saying goodbyes and yet, That is what the teaching art is all about; preparing them for moving on. They're going home for summer now and so am I, to rest, to renew, to once more fill my cup for giving. I'm feeling warm inside knowing well that teaching is a loving craft. We're going home for summer now.

--- *Art Fettig* © ---

Northern Upper Peninsula - Michigan

Teacher's Serenity Prayer

God grant me wisdom, creativity, and love.

With wisdom,
I may look to the future and see the effect
that my teaching will have on these children,
and thus adapt my methods
to fit the needs of each one.

With creativity,
I can prepare new and interesting projects
that can challenge my students
and expand their minds
to set higher goals and dream loftier dreams.

With love,
I can praise my students for jobs well done
and encourage them to get up
and go on when they fail,
Lord reveal yourself through me.
Amen
--- *Author Unknown* ---

Yellowstone Lake - Yellowstone National Park

Teacher, Teacher

Teacher, teacher, help me learn
When to press on, when to turn.
Teacher, teacher, help me grow
Hug me, I need hugging so.

Teacher, teacher, give me hope
Won't you show me how to cope?
Teacher, teacher, guide my way
Teach me what I ought to say.

Teacher, teacher, I'm worthwhile
Won't you give me just one smile?
Teacher, teacher you're so grand
When you help me understand.

Teacher, teacher, when you care
You prove love's a thing we share.
Teacher, teacher, yes it's true
Teacher, teacher, we love you.

--- *Art Fettig ©* **---**

Dent Island - British Columbia

Teaching

Taught my first writing class last night.
I saw the eager look on those faces
and did everything I thought was right
to put the right ideas in the right places.

Enthusiasm, excitement, I acted the elegant Don.
God, how intensely I wanted to turn those people on;
to wake the creative instinct in each of those sleeping souls;
to teach them the power of believing, inspire them to setting goals.

And when my class had ended, I saw some sparks in their eyes.
They looked eager to start writing and my joy I could not disguise.

I taught my first writing class last night
and I learned more than anyone else there.
You can reach people, move them, if you honestly care.

--- Art Fettig © ---

Northern Upper Peninsula - Michigan

"I am a teacher, it is the greatest gift that life could give me, since I am allowed to spend my days with the future of the world. My students will be presidents, doctors, lawyers, craftpersons but hopefully they will all be teachers to someone."

--- *Jack Podojil* © ---

"There is divine beauty in learning, just as there is human beauty in tolerance. To learn means to accept the postulate that life did not begin at my birth. Others have been here before me, and I walk in their footsteps. The books I have read were composed by generations of fathers and sons, mothers and daughters, teachers and disciples. I am the sum total of their experiences, their quests. And so are you."

--- *Elie(zer) Wiesel (b. 1928) --- Romanian-born writer, lecturer, survivor Nazi camps* ---

Siuslaw River - Mapleton, Oregon

"A mother once asked Gandhi to get her son to stop eating sugar. Gandhi told the child, "Come back in two weeks." Two weeks later the mother brought the child before Gandhi. Gandhi said to the boy, "Stop eating sugar." Puzzled the woman replied, "Thank you, but I must ask you why didn't you tell him that two weeks ago?" Gandhi replied, "Two weeks ago I was eating sugar."

--- *Author Unknown* ---

"We ask for strength
And the Great Spirit gives us difficulties,
Which makes us strong."

--- *Native American Prayer* ---

Southern Minnesota - Early Morning

"My heart is singing for joy this morning.
A miracle has happened!
The light of understanding has shone upon my little pupil's mind,
And behold, all things are changed."
--- Anne Sullivan ---

"He who is afraid to ask is ashamed of learning."
--- Danish Proverb ---

"If your plan is for 1 year, plant rice;
If your plan is for 10 years, plant trees;
If your plan is for 100 years, educate children."
--- Confucius ---

Yellowstone Lake - Yellowstone National Park

Whose Child Is This?

"Whose child is this?" I asked one day
Seeing a little one out at play
"Mine", said the parent with a tender smile
"Mine to keep a little while
To bathe his hands and comb his hair
To tell him what he is to wear
To prepare him that he may always be good
And each day do the things he should."

"Whose child is this?" I asked again
As the door opened and someone came in
"Mine", said the teacher with the same tender smile
"Mine, to keep just for a little while
To teach him how to be gentle and kind
To train and direct his dear little mind
To help him live by every rule
And get the best he can from school."

"Whose child is this?" I asked once more
Just as the little one entered the door
"Ours" said the parent and the teacher as they smiled
And each took the hand of the little child
"Ours to love and train together
Ours this blessed task forever."

--- Author Unknown ---

Yellowstone Lake - Yellowstone National Park

"When the pupil is ready, the teacher will come."

--- *Chinese Proverb* ---

"One test of the correctness of educational procedure
is the happiness of the child."

--- *Maria Montessori* ---

"Education would be much more effective if its purpose was to ensure that by the time they leave school every boy and girl should know how much they do not know, and be imbued with a lifelong desire to know it."

--- *Sir William Haley* ---

"I touch the future. I teach."

--- *Christa McAuliffe* ---

Jervis Inlet - British Columbia

Why God Created Teachers

When God created teachers,
He gave us special friends
To help us understand His world
And truly comprehend
The beauty and the wonder
Of everything we see,
And become a better person
With each discovery.

When God created teachers,
He gave us special guides
To show us ways in which to grow
So we can all decide
How to live and how to do
What's right instead of wrong,
To lead us so that we can lead
And learn how to be strong.

Why God created teachers,
In His wisdom and His grace,
Was to help us learn to make our world
A better, wiser place.
--- *Author Unknown* ---

Bryce Canyon - Utah

"Education is an important element in the struggle for human rights. It is the means to help our children and thereby increase self-respect. Education is our passport to the future, for tomorrow belongs to the people who prepare for it today."

--- *Malcolm X* ---

"Act as if what you do makes a difference, because it does."

--- *Author Unknown*---

"The empires of the future are the empires of the mind."

--- *Winston Churchill*---

Yellowstone Lake - Yellowstone National Park

" A teacher affects eternity; he can never tell where his influence stops."

--- Henry Adams, The Education of Henry Adams ---

"Seek for understanding & you will seek no more."

--- Author Unknown ---

"Believe in children, there is faith in their eyes, love in their touch, kindness in their gestures. Thrill with them at life's big and small moments, hold them close."

--- Author Unknown ---

"Even a broken clock is right twice a day."

--- Author Unknown ---

A Teacher's Survival Kit For Everyday Living

" TOOTHPICK-reminds us to look for the good qualities in our students.
You may be the only teacher who says something positive to them that day.

RUBBER BAND-reminds the teacher that they have to be flexible.
Things don't always go the way we plan,
But flexibility will help to work it out.

BAND AID-reminds the teacher that sometimes we do more than teach,
That we help heal hurt feelings, broken dreams,
And lend an ear to a problem.

PENCIL-reminds us to be thankful and we should list our blessings daily,
But also encourage our students to list their blessings
And to be proud of their accomplishments.

ERASER-reminds us to allow students to know we are human
And make mistakes just like they do, and it's ok.
We must all be able to learn from our mistakes.

CHEWING GUM-reminds us to stick with it
And encourage our students to do like wise.
Even the impossible task or assignment can be accomplished
By sticking to it.

MINT-reminds us and our students we are worth a mint.
(We may not be paid a mint, but are worth one.)

CANDY KISS-reminds us that everyone needs a hug,
Kiss, or warm fuzzy everyday.
(All teachers, students, parents, and even administrators)

TEA BAG-reminds us we need time to relax,
Go over our blessings, and take time for others.
Family, husbands, wives, friends, children need quality time together.

A teacher must be willing to show their students how much they care!!!"

--- Original Author Unknown ---
--- Adaptation for teachers by Charles Nelson and his fellow teachers
--- South Carolina ---

Pender Harbor - British Columbia

Teachers

" Teachers are full of patience
Teachers never give up,
And won't let you give up either.
Teachers take students seriously.
Teachers care in their sleep
Teachers see the genius
In every drawing, poem and essay.
Teachers make you feel important.
Teachers also help others.
Teachers never grow old.
Teachers stay famous in their students' minds,
Forever."

--- Author Unknown---

Near Roche Harbor - British Columbia

"Education breeds confidence.
Confidence breeds hope.
Hope breeds peace."
--- Confucius ---

" I will never let my schooling get in the way of my education."
--- Mark Twain ---

" If you treat an individual as he is, he will remain as he is.
But if you treat him as if he were what he ought to be and could be,
He will become what he ought to be and could be."
--- Author Unknown ---

Jackson Lake - Wyoming

"Blessed are those who teach."

--- *Author Unknown* ---

"If the children are untaught, their ignorance and vices will in future life cost us much dearer in their consequences than it would have done in their correction by a good education."

--- *Thomas Jefferson* ---

"In a completely rational society, the best of us would aspire to be teachers and the rest of us would have to settle for something less, because passing civilization along from one generation to the next ought to be the highest honor and the highest responsibility anyone could have."

--- *Lee Iacocca* ---

Beach near Maceio - Brazil

"We can't solve problems
By using the same kind of thinking we used when we created them."
--- Albert Einstein ---

"The human mind is not capable of grasping the Universe.
We are like a little child entering a huge library.
The walls are covered to the ceiling with books in many different tongues.
The child knows that someone must have written these books.
It does not know who or how.
It does not understand the languages in which they are written.
But the child notes a definite plan in the arrangement of the books;
A mysterious order it does not comprehend, but only dimly suspects."
--- Albert Einstein ---

" Lives of great men all remind us

We can make our lives sublime,

And, departing, leave behind us

Footprints on the sands of time."

--- Henry Wadsworth Longfellow ---

"To teach is to learn, again.

People don't care how much you know,

Until they know how much you care.

Remember this when dealing with your students,

Especially with the challenging ones."

--- Author Unknown---

Mineral Pool - Yellowstone National Park

"Teachers who educate children
Deserve more honor than parents who merely gave birth.
For bare life is furnished by the one,
The other ensures a good life."
--- Aristotle---

" No printed page,
No spoken plea,
May teach young hearts,
What men should be.
Not all the books,
On all the shelves,
But what the teachers are themselves."
--- Author Unknown ---

Dent Island - British Columbia

"We worry about what a child will be tomorrow,
Yet forget that he is someone today."

--- *Author Unknown* ---

" Teaching is not a profession, it's a passion."

--- *Author Unknown* ---

Tetons - Wyoming

" At this moment in time, our technology surpasses our humanity.
But when I look at me and you, I now believe that our humanity
Will one day definitely surpass our technology."

--- Albert Einstein ---

" Every child's life is like a piece of paper
On which every person leaves a mark."

--- Chinese Proverb ---

" Minds are like parachutes. They only function when open."

--- *Author Unknown* ---

"In every school classroom, a student should be able to look around and see a model classroom, where there are no safety or health hazards, and where skilled instructors are protecting their safety and health by teaching a professional skill on safe equipment and in a safe environment."

--- *Jack Podojil* © ---

" If you can't imagine it, you can never do it."

--- *Author Unknown* ---

Good Isn't Good Enough !

My Child, beware of "good enough,"
It isn't made of sterling stuff.
It's something anyone can do;
It marks the many from the few.
The flaw which may escape the eye,
And temporarily get by.
Shall weaken underneath the strain,
And wreck the ship, the car, or plane.
With "good enough," the car breaks down,
And one falls short of high renown.
My child, remember and be wise,
In "good enough," disaster lies.

With "good enough," the shirkers stop,
In every factory and shop;
With "good enough," the failures rest,
And lose the one who gives the best.
Who stops at "good enough" shall find,
Success has left them far behind.
For this is true of you and your stuff--
Only the best is "good enough."

--- *Author Unknown* ---

Vancouver - British Columbia

Teacher's Prayer

I want to teach my students
How to live this life on earth
To face its struggles and its strife
And improve their worth

Not just the lesson in a book
Or how the rivers flow
But how to choose the proper path
Wherever they may go

To understand eternal truth
And know the right from wrong
And gather all the beauty
Of a flower and a song

For if I help the world to grow
In wisdom and grace
Then I shall feel that I have won
And I have filled my place

And so I ask your guidance, God
That I may do my part
For character and confidence
And happiness of heart
--- *Author Unknown* ---

Whistler Mountain - British Columbia

"They always say that time changes things,
But you actually have to change them yourself."
--- Andy Warhol ---

" Teachers:
Parents send us their best.
They are entrusting us to make their best-----BETTER!"
--- Author Unknown ---

Yellowstone Lake - Yellowstone National Park

“Anyone who stops learning is old, whether at twenty or eighty.
Anyone who keeps learning stays young.”
---Henry Ford ---

“Awaken people’s curiosity. It is enough to open minds,
do not overload them. Put there just a spark.”
--- Anatole France ---

“Learning is never done without errors and defeat.”
---Vladimir Lenin ---

Desolation Sound - British Columbia

"Upon the subject of education, not presuming to dictate any plan or system respecting it, I can only say that I view it as the most important subject which we as a people may be engaged in."

---Abraham Lincoln ---

"Education...beyond all other devices of human origin, is a great equalizer of conditions of men --the balance wheel of the social machinery...It does better than to disarm the poor of their hostility toward the rich; it prevents being poor."

--- Horace Mann ---